Be Good to Each Other

Other Books by Lowell Erdahl

Pro-Life/Pro-Peace: Life-Affirming Alternatives to Abortion, War, Mercy Killing, and the Death Penalty

The Lonely House: Strength for Times of Loss

Ten for Our Time: A New Look at the Ten Commandments

Be Good to Each Other

An Open Letter on Marriage

Lowell and Carol Erdahl

Augsburg ■ Minneapolis

Library of Congress Cataloging-in-Publication Data

Erdahl, Lowell O.
 Be good to each other : an open letter on marriage / Lowell and Carol Erdahl.
  p. cm.
 Reprint. Originally published: New York : Hawthorn Books, c1976.
 ISBN 0-8066-2541-4
 1. Marriage. 2. Family. I. Erdahl, Carol. II. Title.
[HQ734.E72 1991]
306.8—dc20   91-6334
                       CIP

Manufactured in the U.S.A.   AF 9-2541

99 98 97 96   5 6 7 8 9 10 11 12 13 14 15

To Becky, Paul, and Beth

Contents

Preface   9

1. Dear Pam and John   11

2. Share What Is Deepest   17

3. Marry a Good Friend   29

4. Who Decides What?   39

5. Alone Together   51

6. Getting Out of Old Ruts   61

7. Concerns from Kids to Kinfolk   67

8. Faithfulness in Equal Marriage   79

Questions for Reflection and Discussion   85

Preface

THIS BOOK is a considerably expanded version of a long letter that we sent to Carol's nephew, John, and his bride, Pam, on the occasion of their marriage. It was the longest letter we have ever written, exceeding in length even the longest letters of the apostle Paul. We readily acknowledge that St. Paul was not only more brief but also more profound. Yet we believe there is at least a slight parallel between what we have written to Pam and John and what Paul wrote to the Christians at Rome and other places.

We, too, have sought to share a gift which we hope will be a source of strength and a means toward joy. Being unable to share this gift in person, we, like Paul, chose to put our thoughts in the form of a letter, which enabled us to be personal and yet somewhat comprehensive.

This is, however, no attempt for a final word on marriage. It is one married couple's personal thoughts shared with our nephew and his bride. Since distance kept us from knowing either of them intimately, what we have written may be as meaningful to persons unknown to us as we hope it has been for Pam and John. In this spirit we share our thoughts, hopeful that they may help persons, married or soon to be, find greater joy in the exciting and often perilous venture of life together.

After sending this letter to Pam and John, we made a few copies to share with friends and with couples being married in our church. The response frankly surprised us, resulting in additional copies being run for use in a marriage enrichment series in our congregation and a marriage counseling course at Luther Northwestern Theological Seminary. On the basis of these experiences, we boldly suggest that in addition to being a book for personal reading and for a wedding, anniversary, Christmas, or birthday gift, *Be Good to Each Other* can also be an aid for pastors and counselors in premarital and marriage counseling, marriage enrichment series in churches, and seminary courses and pastoral seminars preparing students and clergy for more effective counseling.

In order to facilitate the kind of communication we believe essential to meaningful marriage, we have added an appendix of questions and thoughts for reflection and discussion. We hope that couples will use these thoughts and questions in their private discussions and that church groups and counseling classes will find in them a concrete basis for group discussion.

All will not agree with everything we have written, but we hope that the reading of it will stimulate reflection and communication. If some through these pages find more meaning in marriage, we will be grateful.

1

Dear Pam
and John

*D*ear Pam and John,
    As you begin your venture of marriage, we want to give you a personal gift. We have never shared a gift in this way before, but we do so now in the hope that it will be meaningful to you. We would like to tell you some of our experiences in marriage, and we wish to share a little of what our years of married life have taught us.

Although we have known you all your life, John, and enjoyed meeting you, Pam, we really don't know either of you very well. Space has kept us apart, but we hope that these thoughts will help to bring us closer and that they will encourage you to live more intimately and joyfully with one another.

We Wish You Joy

Our wish for you is joy abounding through all your years together. This joy includes, but goes beyond, fun and happiness. It is also the joy of tender intimacy shared in body, mind, and spirit. Freedom has a place in it—freedom to grow as persons and as a couple. This joy also includes the sense of meaning that springs from having resources to live from and purposes worth living for. All these, and whatever more goes into joy in fullness, we wish for you.

Our hope and prayer is that a long time from now you will be able to look back across your years together with an abundance of gratitude and a minimum of regret. At best there is, in each of our lives, plenty to regret—all those words and deeds that should, or should never, have been. After over thirty years together, we have memories enough of things we now wish had been different, but in spite of all that, we remain deeply grateful for having shared this time together. Such gratitude seems to us the true sign of joy. So may your adventure of life together lead increasingly to thankfulness that tells of joy.

We Promise You Trouble

Lest there be any misunderstanding, we must go on at once to promise you trouble. We don't know exactly what you expect of marriage, but on the basis of our experience, we will risk a double prediction. First, you will have many times in your marriage when you are so tender, warm, loving, and affectionate that you will doubt you could ever again have an unkind thought or feeling toward each other. Second, there will also be times when you are so angry, hurt, and resentful that you will wonder how you could ever have loved each other at all.

On the occasion of his golden wedding anniversary, one of our uncles confided, "During all these fifty years, we have never thought of separation or divorce, but we have on occasion thought of murder."

That, too, has been our experience, and to acknowledge it is not to report a bad marriage. It is, however, to confess a relationship in which affection and anger, joy and resentment, fun and frustration follow and precede each other within the changing cycles of intimacy. So when trouble comes, please don't think quickly of separation or divorce, and certainly don't yield to the temptation of murder. Having problems doesn't necessarily mean that you have an unsatisfactory marriage; it can mean that you have an intimate marriage.

A friend once told us, "It's terrible to be married." He defended this statement by pointing to some of the heavy responsibilities and limits of freedom that marriage involves. He told of resentments and misunderstandings that can make marriage miserable. But then, lest we get the wrong impression, he went on to say, "It's also wonderful to be married. It is the most meaningful, joyful relationship that I have ever had, and I would not change it for anything."

We have often thought of how his experience is equally true in other ways. It is both terrible and wonderful to be single; there are miseries and joys in the single life. So also with being human, it is both terrible and wonderful to be alive in this world. Across the years both gloom and gladness are part of every person's experience.

Marriage Can't Do Everything

We know from experience that living together can create changes for better and worse. Because we are so important to each other, we do more than anyone else to lift or depress each other's moods. Marriage solves some problems but creates others. Someone has said that "Half the troubles of life come from being single and the other half from being married." We certainly understand the point but don't think it's quite true.

In terms of percentages, it seems more likely that about 25 percent of the problems come from being single and 25 percent from being married, with the other 50 percent coming from being alive in a world like ours. That is to say, we think that at least half our troubles have little to do with whether we are single or married. They are just part of what is involved in being human. Failure to recognize this fact may be one of the most significant contributors to unhappy and broken marriages.

When we get married, it's easy to dream of marriage as the solution to all our problems. But this is an illusion. Getting married will, hopefully, solve some problems, but it will not automatically free us from the troubles that come with being human. We still have to face the routines of daily living. We are still as susceptible as ever to the basic anxieties of existence which remind us that we are not gods, but human beings—frail, finite, fallible—who one day sooner or later will die.

Those who get married in the hope of being freed from all the anxieties of human existence are certain to be disappointed. When the realities of married life destroy this dream, they may think that the fault is in this particular marriage. They may begin to fantasize over being married to someone else who could make the dream come true. There are, of course, mistaken marriages, and for some the "second time around" is more beautiful than the first. But when this is so, the couple may have entered into the marriage with more realistic expectations. Neither getting married, nor getting divorced, nor getting remarried solves the basic problems of human life. They are always present.

A good marriage will make our problems easier to bear, and a bad marriage will likely make them seem worse. But let's neither blame everything on, nor credit everything to, marriage. The fault or blessing often lies, not in our marital state but in ourselves and in our wider world.

To stress that marriage can't do everything is not to deny its immense potential for good. Being legally bound to each other so that we cannot call off the relationship on a moment's notice facilitates more joy than misery. The legal obligations about which we may complain keep us together through troubled times, enabling us again to be renewed in love.

We believe that Dietrich Bonhoeffer overstates the case when he says, "It is not your love that sustains the marriage, but from now on, the marriage that sustains your love." Our marriage is certainly sustained by our love, but the reverse is also true: our love *is* sustained by our marriage.

Forewarned Is Forearmed

We hope that you expect great gladness in your life together. Joy waits to sustain you and to surprise you. But to be forewarned of difficult days can help you see your marriage in a more mature perspective.

Whether single or married, there will always be hard times ahead. Accepting the fact that life will not always be easy, can strangely help to make things a lot easier for us. For example, understanding that the "model" teenager is often a bit rebellious can help parents live more comfortably through those turbulent years. In the same way, awareness that the "model" marriage includes normal, human ups and downs as well as the inevitable conflicts that come with closeness, helps us to adjust and to recover more quickly. Human life is an often lonely voyage on a restless sea. We are tremendously grateful that we can sail together, but have learned that our love does not shield us from every turbulent wind and wave.

When you encounter your first serious conflicts and see each other at your worst, you will be tempted to say, "Now I see what you are really like! You are mean and selfish." But wait a minute! You will have seen and said the truth. All of us are mean and selfish. That's a fact of life. It's true, but it's not all the truth. That isn't all that we are "really like." We are also loving and kind. We are capable of great love as well as great hatred. To face that double fact in ourselves as well as in our partner is a step toward mature intimacy.

Our most happy moments are saddened by an awareness that this time of ecstasy will pass. Occasions of deepest communion with one another will be followed sooner or later by times of conflict and misunderstanding. But the other side is also true. Times of resentment and coldness will be followed by reconciliation and warm renewal. It's been said that "married couples go from the world war to the *boudoir*" and vice versa. Those transitions don't always happen quickly, but that they do happen is an indication of the dynamic changes of attitude and action that are part of living together in married life.

Growing marriages live by what someone has called "the multiple honeymoon plan." When bad days come and you wonder if the honeymoon is over, do not despair. Get busy planning for another honeymoon— either at home or at a not-too-expensive place nearby.

2

Share What
Is Deepest

*J*ess Lair, in his book *I Ain't Much Baby—but I'm All I've Got* says, "The most loving thing we can do is tell it like it is with us in our deepest hearts." Someone else has said, "To love is to give yourself to someone else." Those definitions go together. To tell what is in our deepest hearts is to give ourselves to someone else.

In our experience, the deepest intimacy of marriage is not the intimacy of sexual relations. They are a wonderful and vital part of total intimacy. Praise God for this beautiful gift! But even more intimate than the physical closeness of sexual relations is the mental and emotional sharing of mind and heart. To share the depths of our minds and hearts, to confide our hopes and fears and doubts and dreams is intimacy at its best.

Such sharing is often painful and sometimes embarrassing. The depths contain thoughts of dread and disappointment which we do not like to admit to ourselves or to confide to someone else. To our rational minds many of the things that bother us seem either too personal or too insignificant to talk about. We may think we are too big to be upset by such things. But our feelings are not ruled by our minds, and often the only way to clear the air and renew the relationship is to talk it out. Talk can be cheap, but it can also be priceless. To share the negative as well as the positive is the painful price of intimacy. As we open up to each other, we experience the truth of the old saying, "When we share our joys, we double them; when we share our troubles, we cut them in half."

"He Doesn't Talk to Me"

A wife once explained the problem in her marriage. She first bragged about her husband. He was an excellent provider, faithful and kind. He was good with the children, and she had no doubt of his love. "There is just one little thing," she said. "He doesn't talk to me."

Subsequent conversation revealed that wasn't literally true. He did talk about some things. He said, "Please pass the potatoes" and "What movie would you like to see tonight?" He talked about painting the house and going to the ball game. But he did not share what was in his deepest heart. He didn't confide his personal thoughts or feelings. As the months and years passed, she began to feel as if she were living with a stranger.

Sharing in depth seems especially difficult for some people who have been brought up in families where they keep everything to themselves. Some men seem to feel that telling personal thoughts and feelings is a sign of weakness or a threat to their manhood. Even to say, "I love you" is to confess the need of another person, which some, in their fear of becoming dependent, find difficult.

Yet whatever our past patterns of isolation, something in us yearns for a relationship in which we can be open and honest with each other. While inhibitions keep us from sharing freely, yearnings for intimacy invite us to risk saying something to help break the defensive wall that keeps us a lonely stranger separated from the one we love.

There are ways in which these defenses can be broken. The woman who complained that "he doesn't talk to me" finally told her husband of her anguish. To her surprise he agreed to visit with a counselor, in whose presence they were able to make a new beginning in their relationship. She learned that there were some ways in which she contributed to her husband's silence and others by which she made it easier for him to be more open.

We sometimes encourage and enable the very behavior and attitudes in each other that we most dislike. We may, for example, complain about silent partners and yet so ridicule their attempts at sharing that they feel put down and retreat into solitude. It's safer.

Sometimes, while complaining of too much nagging and bickering, we continue doing all sorts of things that provoke it.

Let's Talk about It

If you are having difficulty sharing, here are two communication starters that some people have found helpful.

The first deals with personal role expectations. Each of us expects certain things of ourselves and of our spouses. Some are more important than others. To help each other know what matters most to you, try arranging the following items in order of importance:

____ to help earn the family income

____ to take some responsibility for meals and house-keeping

____ to seek common recreational and cultural interests

____ to be a satisfying sexual partner

____ to maintain good relations with relatives and friends

____ to care for the children

____ to be a personal companion

____ to promote correct religious faith and values

____ to manage the family finances

____ to take a leadership role in community and social activities

____ to assume the major responsibility for making family decisions

Make two lists. In the first, list them in order of importance for yourself; in the second, in terms of what you expect of your spouse. Don't attempt to guess what you think your partner's order of importance will be. Let your spouse do that for himself or herself.

Do this ranking independently. Add other areas that are important to you; then compare and talk about the things that are most significant to each of you and why. This is not a test. Try to be as honest as possible. If your number one expectation of your spouse is his or her number ten expectation of self, you had better face the difference and seek mutually satisfying accommodation or compromise.

We don't have to agree on everything but we do need to come to terms with our differences. One spouse can like western music while the other prefers classics. But if you have only one stereo, you can't play both at the same time. Equal marriage at its best gives each partner freedom to be oneself while respecting the limits of freedom inherent in a love relationship.

A wife and mother once said, "We hold each other tightly with an *open* hand." To us that open hand is a beautiful symbol of love which does hold tightly but does not stifle or enslave.

"I Like It When . . ."

As another conversation starter we suggest use of a simple, but significant sentence completion exercise. Thinking in terms of your relationship, complete the sentence "I like it when . . ." in ten different ways. Then share your sentences with each other and talk about why you feel as you do. Such grateful sharing reinforces the positive aspects of your relationship. For maximum benefit use "I like it when . . ." sentences as part of your daily conversation. Whether in response to a bit of spice added literally to a meal or figuratively to some other event in your life together, these "I like it when . . ." comments will help keep you going and growing.

As your communication deepens, you will discover both your differences and your similarities. You will sometimes be surprised that you both feel rejected or dominated by each other. When you find yourself saying, "What do you mean? You are the one who's been ignoring me!" you have discovered a common feeling that can help you grow in your understanding of each other. By exploring this shared feeling together, you can further deepen your relationship.

Say It and Hear It

When we husbands and wives fail to understand each other, it is likely because we are remiss in speaking or listening or both. We may, for example, complain of being misunderstood and yet be guilty ourselves for having shared too little to be understood.

Spouses in marital counseling commonly say to each other, "I never knew you felt that way" or "Why didn't you tell me that before?" It would often be helpful to be able to read each other's minds, but until we have developed that art more fully, we need to speak our minds and hearts.

On the other hand, speaking produces no understanding until it is heard. Most of us are better at speaking than listening. We need to be reminded of the old saying, "The good Lord has given each of us two ears and one mouth, and we should take the hint." Too often we talk much and hear little; and even when silent, we are more preoccupied with what we are planning to say next than attentive to what the other is saying. So when we complain that we don't, or can't, understand our partners, *we* may have failed to hear what was clearly expressed.

Speech and hearing are great gifts but are of no value until they are used. We need not feel sorry for ourselves for being misunderstood or for being incapable of understanding each other. As we have mouths to speak and ears to hear, we can use them.

Take time to verbalize. If that doesn't come naturally, prepare a little speech or write a letter. Take time to listen with attention and concern for what is really being said. If it is not clear, ask your spouse, "What do you mean?" We are often surprised at what we learn. More than that, we help each other to fulfill one of our deepest human needs—the need to be understood.

When we listen, we may hear some things over and over. We may be tempted to shut off the conversation with a sarcastic "You told me that before." But why do these things keep coming up? Is it because we still haven't heard them? Do they express something significant?

This may be especially true of childhood memories. These may seem like meaningless incidents, but there are reasons why they keep coming to mind and why we feel it necessary to share them with someone else. When we tell these memories, we are really saying, "I want you to know me and to understand why I am as I am."

The Wrong Fears

There are some things we are afraid to share because we do not wish to burden each other. Perhaps we have troubles at work, but to tell about them would cause worry and anxiety. There are times when we must keep things to ourselves, yet not to share them may create isolation. There is a tremendous feeling of separation when we sense that our spouse is troubled but does not trust or respect us enough to share it.

At other times we decline from sharing for fear that we will reveal our weakness. If we start to cry we may expose ourselves to ridicule, so we don't dare talk about it. We clam up and cry on the inside or cry when we are alone, which is probably far better than not at all.

In our society men are especially inhibited in this regard, but if women are learning to honestly assert their minds and wills, men can also be liberated to honestly express their emotions. Tears and laughter are gifts of God, and when there is something to cry or laugh about, it is good to cry and to laugh.

Often we are afraid of the wrong things. We are afraid to show our emotions though hiding them keeps us from meeting and understanding each other. We are afraid that our walls of defense will fall down though these very walls separate us from one another. To share times of tears as well as laughter is part of the pain and joy of intimacy.

We all yearn for a marriage relationship in which we can be totally open and honest with each other, and we should do all we can to make such sharing possible. But we also need to remember that honesty isn't everything. We need to be kind as well as truthful.

In kindness we will sometimes choose to keep some truth to ourselves. When, for example, we meet someone more beautiful or more handsome than our spouse, we don't need to rush home declaring, "I wish you were as good-looking as so-and-so I met today." It might be true, but it certainly would not be kind. While "speaking the truth in love," we are to "be kind to one another, tenderhearted" (Eph. 4:15, 32).

What Are You Trying to Tell Me?

Even couples who seldom verbalize their deepest thoughts and feelings are still constantly communicating with each other. Their attitudes and actions speak more loudly than their words. Almost everything we do or say has some meaning if we can only see or hear what it is.

A concerned farmer rushed across the field to ask his neighbor why he was beating his mule. "I'm not beating him," the neighbor replied, "I'm just trying to get his attention." In similar ways we do all sorts of things to get each other's attention. If we realize this, we can be much more understanding and considerate of each other's behavior and attitudes.

Once, as a couple was in the middle of an intense argument, the wife viciously berated her husband. When the counselor asked, "What are you trying to tell him?" the woman's mood changed abruptly, and she began to cry. Through the tears she blurted, "I just wish that once in a while he'd take me in his arms and tell me that he loves me." Until that moment her husband probably was not getting the message. All he heard was anger and resentment, yet his wife was pleading for love.

We may criticize this wife for not simply saying to her husband, "Tell me that you love me." But when we think about it, we know why she was reluctant. She lived in the hope that he would say it without being asked. Had he come home and given her a big hug after having been asked, she would have thought, "You're only doing it because I asked you." Having waited so long, only in painful desperation could she finally blurt it out. Sometime before, when the emotional pitch was less intense, had they been able to share their mutual longings in a setting like that of the "I like it when . . ." exercise, they might have been able to avoid this conflict.

We urge you to listen for the sounds of the heart as well as the lips and to look behind your actions for their possible meanings. Ask each other, "What are you trying to tell me?" When you do, we think you will often discover what someone has called "the soul of goodness" behind the appearance of evil. Our worst words and most hurtful behavior are often cries of desperation that rise from God-given but frustrated yearnings for love and life.

Accentuate the Positive

When we were young, there was a popular song titled "Ac-Cent-Tchu-Ate the Positive," which also encouraged elimination of the negative. We think it is neither wise nor possible to eliminate all negative thoughts and do not advocate a Pollyanna approach to life. At the same time, we have learned that it is better to accentuate the positive than harp on the negative.

A wise coach was once asked why he did so little complaining about the team's mistakes and so much bragging about their good plays. He replied, "I have discovered that complaining doesn't do much good and that commending does much to create a better team." So also with life in general. Who are the people who have most influenced your life for good? Are they persons who have given you the most criticism or those who have provided the most encouragement?

Imagine a marriage in which negative comments abound: "Why can't you ever be on time?" "Don't you know how to do anything right?" "You are about as sexless as they come!" Do you think such comments improve punctuality, household repairs, and sexual fulfillment? If anything, they are likely to create resentment, which only makes the problem worse.

Imagine another marriage in which the couple make a point of sharing positive appreciation. An honestly spoken "I am glad you are home early," or "The bedroom looks beautiful; you painted it like a pro," or a tenderly whispered "I think you are very sexy" will do more to encourage the same behavior than will a month of griping.

You may be thinking, "Wait a minute; in the first example things were terrible, so there was nothing to be positive about. In the other all was well, so it was natural to be appreciative." Maybe, but maybe not. How did these marriages get this way? They may have begun with similar circumstances, but harping created resentment that reinforced negative behavior in the one, while appreciation encouraged positive behavior in the other.

To urge accentuation of the positive is not to advocate dishonesty or manipulative game playing but rather to promote honest expression of heartfelt appreciation. The positive couple didn't just pretend or make up things for which to be grateful. When they saw a good thing, they were simply honest and kind enough to acknowledge it.

Even when a couple is coexisting in a state of cold-war isolation, they usually continue to be halfway civilized toward each other so that there are some things for which to be rightly grateful. If each would be honest enough to confess a little thankfulness such as "That was really a good dinner" or "Thanks for picking up the back hall," there might be a breakthrough toward a much better life together.

Being properly positive also means having the kindness to express complaints with tact and to realize that there are times when complaints are better kept to oneself at least temporarily.

Benjamin Franklin recommended that prior to marriage we should have our eyes wide open to see what we are getting into, but after marriage we should keep our eyes half shut to overlook a lot of little faults that aren't worth being troubled about.

Edward Everett Hale made the same point when he said, "Make it your habit not to be critical about small things."

A woman visited a psychotherapist, seeking help in dealing with her parents-in-law, with whom she and her husband were living. The therapist advised her to be more open in expressing her feelings. She went home and "told everyone off," including her husband. The problem became worse than ever. Now she had an angry husband and a couple of bewildered and rejected parents to deal with. Fortunately, they all had the maturity to face the situation and make a new beginning.

Their experience should not lead us to bottle everything up, but it can remind us that impulsively blowing our stacks is seldom an automatic cure for all our problems.

Tact expresses both the love and friendship that characterize a healthy marital relationship. Although some may sing, "This is the end of a beautiful friendship, this is the beginning of love," we believe that love and friendship go together.

The Bible tells of a young woman who says of the one she loves, "This is my beloved, and this is my friend" (Song of Solomon 5:16). We hope that your relationship will continue to grow so that you will always be able to say those words of each other.

3

Marry a
Good Friend

*A*nn Landers urges people looking toward a meaningful lifelong relationship to "marry a good friend." Being good friends is an insufficient basis for marriage, but friendship is necessary for a lasting relationship of mutual understanding and joy. To say this is not to minimize the romantic side of marriage. Most people would agree that they should marry someone with whom they could enjoy going to bed, but some seem less concerned about marrying a person with whom they could enjoy getting up in the morning.

One problem with premarital sex is that it can easily short-circuit the relationship so that, while there may be much passion, there is little chance for the development of friendship. Passion and friendship seem best kept together. The combined sharing of the heart, mind, and body enriches intimacy at every level.

Our writing to you now about marrying a good friend may seem inappropriate. Whatever your motives for courtship, you are now getting married, so isn't it a bit late to think of these things? We don't think so. Even if passion has overshadowed friendship thus far, it is not too late to become good friends. Friendship begins and thrives as it is nurtured by sharing mutual concerns. It enhances rather than diminishes the potential for passionate fulfillment.

We certainly have had some unfriendly times but are immensely grateful that on most days we are able to name each other as "my best friend." There is no magic in how this happens; it is part of the overall effect of everything we think, do, feel, and say. Remember that friendship is based on *mutual* respect.

Some marriages seem founded upon neurotic dependencies rather than mutual respect. One may, for example, feel sorry for the other and mistake the sense of being needed for being in love. The other may worship the needed one as a kind of savior without whom he or she cannot possibly live. Pity is a virtue, but it is a poor basis for marriage. Making a god of another person also sets the stage for disillusionment.

No one can be a god to anyone else. It is both disastrous and idolatrous to try. As God does not take the place of a person who dies but leaves an empty place, as if in tribute to that person's importance, so also a spouse does not take the place of God. We can't be gods or saviors for each other, but we can be friends. We can share our lives as human beings who both respect and need, but do not worship or rely solely upon, each other. Being someone, but not everything, to each other, we live in a healthy interdependence, feeling free to give and receive without demeaning or idolizing.

There are, no doubt, many mutually satisfying marriages that exist without the intimacy of deep friendship. These husbands and wives live together as practical business partners, cooperating in daily responsibilities while relating to each other with respect and care but without much intellectual or emotional communication. Some have other best friends with whom they can share in an openness and mutual understanding which seems impossible in their marriage. Others appear able to live contentedly as private persons who have no in-depth friendships.

When both husband and wife are happy with such an arrangement, we are grateful they found each other, but it would be difficult for either of us to find fulfillment in such a marriage. For us the sharing of intimate friendship is vital for our life together. If you are like us, we wish it also for you.

Pulling on the Beans

Every farmer knows that you can't make beans grow by pulling on them. But many of us strain our marital friendship by trying to force change in one another. We may be able to forcibly change someone's behavior, but it's doubtful that pressure has much positive effect upon our attitudes or long-range living patterns.

Coercion can often be counterproductive. When we sense that someone is out to change us, we tend to dig in our heels and become more stubborn than ever. On the other hand, when we sense that we are loved and accepted as we are, we are free to let down our defenses and open the doors to change. Beyond that fact, no person has the right to enslave another. My spouse is not *my* possession to control but God's gift to love.

Adopting such attitudes of acceptance is especially difficult for those who are idealists. It is wonderful to have high standards and noble goals, but if they are beyond human attainment, they can become tyrants that drive us to despair and our partners to depart. We all need what someone has called "the courage of imperfection," which recognizes that we are imperfect people living in an imperfect world.

Some people are so oppressed by the tyranny of an impossible ideal that they miss the happiness at hand because it does not compare with the imaginary joy of their dreams. Persons who flit from marriage to marriage like a bee from flower to flower are probably the victims of such dreams. They lack the frustration tolerance necessary to endure the pain of intimacy. When the relationship begins to hurt, they fail to realize that the anguish may be the birth pangs of intimacy.

We hope you will have the wisdom and courage to endure in order to find the deeper meaning and more profound happiness that lie beyond the pain. Such endurance is a vital part of being a good friend.

Be Good to Each Other

The best marriage advice some friends of ours ever received came not from the pastor who performed their wedding but from a gas station attendant along their honeymoon route. All he said was, "Be good to each other," but it made a deep impression on the newlyweds, and we have pondered it often.

Being good to each other, you will seek to give joy as well as get it. You will try to do all you can to make your partner happy and will not be constantly preoccupied with "what's in it for me?" When a husband and wife think almost exclusively in terms of what they can get from each other, they will both be miserable. But when they think and act in terms of what they can give to each other, they will both be happy. Because sickness and misery can strike any life, we can't guarantee happiness to anyone, but couples who do all they can to bring joy to each other are generally far happier than husbands and wives who seek only to get joy for themselves.

Jesus' general principle that "those who want to save their life will lose it, and those who lose their life for my sake will save it" (Luke 9:24) is also true in marriage. When we lose ourselves in the abandonment of self-giving love, we discover a meaning and joy which is possible in no other way. We are created to love and to be loved. We find our deepest joy in giving joy to others.

When a gift is given, it needs to be received and acknowledged. Some of us have less trouble giving than receiving. We can generously share ourselves but are too proud to let others give much to us. We probably fear that receiving something will obligate us to someone else and make us more dependent upon that person. But marriage is a relationship of interdependence. We do need each other. To be the proud giver without being a grateful receiver often indicates a self-righteous superiority, which in the long run limits mutual growth and fulfillment.

Mutual giving and receiving are part of the healthy rhythm of marriage. Mature partners are not afraid to ask gifts of each other, nor do they spare their expressions of gratitude. Words of appreciation are a vital part of the language of love. There are a hundred ways of saying thank you, and we do well to use them all, remembering that one of the best is simply to say it. To do so is not to be flatteringly phony, but openly honest in response to another person's goodness to us.

"I'm Sorry, Honey"

Being good to each other also means that we can admit that we *aren't* always good to each other. We believe the three most important expressions in marriage are, first, "I love you," second, "Thank you," and third, "I'm sorry." We do not believe that "love means never having to say you're sorry."

There are many nonverbal ways in which we confess our failures to one another and receive assurance of continued love, but there are also times to *say it*. Someone has pointed out that when husband and wife have an argument, each may feel 100 percent right and regard the other as 100 percent wrong. But when one exercises the kindness and honesty to say to the other, "Honey, I think I was 2 percent wrong," the argument is often 100 percent over.

It is as difficult to be 100 percent right as it is to be 100 percent wrong. When we are wrong it is right to confess it.

After a foolish deed by his child, an angry father berated the child. "Don't be so damn stupid," he said. Several hours later he returned to ask the child's forgiveness. "You are not stupid," he said, "and I should not have talked to you that way. Please forgive me." Neither such criticism nor such confession were the father's daily habit, but his action now stands in the now-grown child's memory as a profound Christian example.

Too often, whether in relation to parents and children or husbands and wives, we think that to be a Christian example we have to be able to say, "Look at me, I'm perfect." Such arrogance is not Christian at all. True Christian example says, "I am far from perfect and need both the forgiveness of God and the forgiveness of those with whom I live."

We are often wrong in our attitudes though right in our opinions. Our facts may be straight while our attitudes are crooked. Many a marriage has ended in misery because one or both partners were so stubbornly committed to being right that the whole relationship went wrong. We need to beware of the arrogance that can win many arguments while destroying the marriage. We may need to choose between being right and being married.

Confession is contagious. When we risk admitting our faults, we free our partner to do the same. Admitting that "I didn't make myself clear" opens the way for the other to acknowledge, "I may not have listened carefully." When one of us says, "I'm sorry I lost my temper this morning," the other can more easily reply, "I guess I had it coming for complaining so much before breakfast."

There is something humorous as well as pathetic in Jesus' story about the man who was forgiven a huge debt and then refused to forgive someone who owed him only a few dollars (Matt. 18:23-35). Seeing ourselves in that parable can help us understand the forgiveness we need to give in light of the forgiveness we need to receive. It can free us from self-righteousness. Gratitude, self-awareness, and a sense of humor can help us become both forgiven and forgiving. That spirit of forgiveness is an important part of being good to each other. Ephesians 4:32 sums it up when it says, "Be kind to one another, tender-hearted, forgiving one another, as God in Christ has forgiven you."

Break the Vicious Cycle

None of us responds with kindness all the time. We are greedy and grasping as well as giving and good. When we are hurt by our partner, we are tempted to pull back our love and retaliate in kind. Such retaliation may start a vicious cycle of recrimination and revenge that must be broken if a relationship of giving and receiving love is to be restored.

Those of us who have experienced God's self-giving and forgiving love are enabled to continue being good to those who are often less than good to us. Because we have received undeserved love, we can hardly stop loving someone who is sometimes unkind to us.

Specific steps toward breaking the vicious cycle are often difficult to take. Upset by numerous marital hurts, one woman, whose husband liked homemade bread, vowed never to bake bread for him again. But after some days of reflection, she decided to be kind to him even if he were mean to her. She baked the bread, and the serving of it became a sign and sacrament of reconciliation. She broke the vicious cycle. The wheel began to turn in the other direction. As meanness had followed meanness and hurt had followed hurt, a kind deed opened the way for kindness in return. Baking a few loaves of bread is not the solution to all marital problems; but when caught in a cycle of meanness, one of us needs to do something that says, "Let's stop this nonsense and try to start a new cycle of kindness and love."

Be Angry!

Many people are surprised that the words *be angry* are in the Bible, but here they are: "Be angry but do not sin; do not let the sun go down on your anger" (Eph. 4:26). Those words come only a few verses before the passage that says, "Be kind to one another" (v. 32), and they remind us of the sometimes difficult problem of expressing our hostile feelings.

Being good to each other means sharing love and affection, and includes saying, "Thank you," "I love you," and "I'm sorry." But it also means having the honesty and courage to say, "I'm angry!"

The people closest to us have the greatest potential for both helping and hurting us. Most of us can thank God for blessings received from our parents, but since

36

none has had perfect parents, we all have scars on our psyches as a result of their mistaken attitudes and actions. So also in marriage, we both help and hurt each other, and occasions of gratitude merge with times of anger.

Some of us "nice guys" may be reluctant to admit our angry feelings even to ourselves, but they will be expressed in one way or another. We may think we are above making an emotional outburst or may think that we can't do anything about it anyway, but serious hostility is not disposed of so easily.

A man who was hospitalized with ulcers and related psychosomatic problems told of being utterly frustrated in trying to deal with the pastor of his church. "There isn't a thing I can do about it," he complained. But the fact is, he did do something about it. He got sick! When we don't handle negative feelings constructively, they work on us like a corrosive acid, poisoning both our bodies and our relationships.

"It Makes Me Mad!"

It's fascinating to observe various ways in which people express anger. Many retreat into silence; some scream and swear, rant or cry; others act out their anger by slamming doors or throwing something. Many of these patterns may have been learned from the families in which we grew up. Though sometimes ashamed, we may feel at home with our way of reacting, even if we dislike it in others.

But what happens when a silent type marries a screamer or a screamer marries a thrower? At worst the marriage may end in murder or divorce, but even at best a difficult adjustment must be made. Talking with each other in calm moments about how we usually respond in times of hurt and resentment can be of great help in understanding each other. You can even learn from each other. If you are silent, you may learn to let go and say something. If you have a short fuse and regret your explosions five minutes afterward, you can learn to count to one hundred instead of to ten.

In any case, it is usually safe to confess *your* feelings without accusing the other. To say, "What you did makes me angry" is a factual description of how you feel. To call your spouse a stupid idiot is, to say the least, less than helpful. The former opens the gates of conversation; the latter slams the door in your partner's face.

There are times when we are so out of touch with our own feelings that we may express our anger in ways only indirectly related to the specific irritation. A wife resentful over her husband's infatuation with sports on TV may discover that she has a headache at bedtime. The husband, angry with his wife's bed time headache, may forget to take out the garbage the next day.

We often catch ourselves behaving in such ways and continue to work at being more honest with each other. Although it's always tempting to express the anger indirectly or fly into a rage or retreat into a sulk, we've learned that it's usually wiser to say, "It makes me mad!" and then take time to talk it through. We've also found it best to follow the biblical admonition, "Do not let the sun go down on your anger" (Eph. 4:26). We try to verbalize our feelings as soon as possible following the offending incident. Doing this makes it easier for us to be angry without hurting ourselves or each other. It also eliminates those awful times of sulking and silence.

4

Who Decides What?

*L*ike all married couples, we have had our difficulties in making decisions. Who decides what? What if we simply can't agree? Does the husband then get to make the final decision?

Some couples say that they try to decide things jointly, but when they reach an impasse, the husband, as "head of the house," chooses the course of action that the wife and children agree to obey. Families with wise and loving husbands may live harmoniously with this arrangement. When the wife is the submissive "heart of the house," willingly yielding responsibility for major decisions to a kind and sensitive husband who rules firmly and yet gently, order and harmony can result. The wife may feel relieved to be free from ultimate responsibility, and the husband's ego may be enhanced by his sense of authority and leadership.

Head and Heart?

But in spite of all that can be said for it, we have not adopted this "head and heart" arrangement. To us it suggests that the husband has all the brains, and the wife all the emotions. We believe that the functions of "head" and "heart" should be shared by both husband and wife. There is much sharing in families that affirm the traditional head-heart roles. Some wives with subtle brilliance literally "rule the roost" while giving their husbands the illusion of doing so. But we have chosen a different process of decision making than the arrangement of "when we can't agree it's up to him."

Being male does not ensure the presence of either love or wisdom. Under "the husband rules" arrangement, wives with superior judgment sometimes are condemned to live under the tyranny of arrogant folly. Even the husband with exceptional brilliance can be in error, and to be committed in advance to his every decision is a dangerous business. Beyond the wisdom of particular decisions, a wife who yields total responsibility for ultimate decision making abdicates something essential to her full personhood and gives her husband responsibility he should not have to bear alone.

Other Arrangements

Another method of decision making is to let the wife have the final say in everything. Needless to say, we don't endorse this either. In our opinion the fact that many would ridicule such a matriarchal arrangement while applauding the patriarchal one is one measure of the unconscious relegation of women to an inferior status in our society.

One step toward greater equality is for husbands and wives to freely yield authority for final decision making to each other in specified areas. The husband with expertise in mechanical matters can, for example, choose the make of the family car, while the wife with greater sensitivity to color combinations is free to decorate the house. While this procedure seems to work well for some couples and is no doubt part of the unspoken contract of every harmonious marriage, we think it is a second-best arrangement. In practice it is often inequitable. The husband may get to decide the place of residence, which is of course the area in which he can get the best job, and the wife can help pick the house and have almost full say in selecting the wallpaper. At the opposite extreme, the husband has full authority to decide what movies they watch on T.V., while the wife decides how they spend their money.

Not Who's Right? but What's Right?

The trouble with arrangements that give final authority to one spouse or try to divide the responsibility in some pre-agreed fashion is that both are based on "Who is right?" rather than "What is right?" In a relationship of mutual respect and love the important thing is not "Whose idea is it?" but "Is it the best idea?" To decide "What's right?" without being able to fall back on either "It's up to me" or "It's up to you" can be frustrating. But just as a democracy, though less efficient, is better for a country than dictatorship, we believe it is also better for a family.

Some Tests of Right and Wrong

There is no simple, fail-safe method of always knowing what's right and what's wrong, but there are some tests to keep in mind as we make significant choices. We

41

urge you to reflect upon the following and discuss them together:

_____ The law test: Is the contemplated action in accordance with the Ten Commandments?

_____ The Golden Rule test: Is it in accordance with the Golden Rule: "Do unto others as you would have them do unto you?"

_____ The test of Jesus' new commandment: Is it in accordance with Jesus' new commandment to "love one another as I have loved you?"

_____ The test of consequences: Is it hurtful or helpful to myself and others?

_____ The test of publicity: Is it something I'd be pleased to have everyone know about?

_____ The test of respected people: Is it something I'd like those whom I respect most to know about?

_____ The test of universality: Would the world be better or worse if everyone were to act in the way I'm thinking of acting?

_____ The test of projected retrospect: Will I likely be pleased five/ten years from now to have done what I'm thinking of doing today?

_____ The test of Jesus' example: Is it something Jesus would do?

_____ The test of self-love: If I do this will I be caring as much for others as I care for myself?

_____ The test of conscience: Will I feel regret or gratitude after the deed is done or left undone?

It might be helpful for each of you to arrange this list in order of importance to you and then talk with each other about why you have placed them as you did.

These tests relate directly to decisions with moral implications, but some are also helpful in answering questions which are less ethical in nature, such as "Where should we live?" or "What kind of car should we buy?"

To illustrate the way in which these tests work in practice, think of the following examples of the application of the test of projected retrospect.

Suppose that husband or wife, while away at a convention, is tempted toward a short-term affair, which could probably be kept secret. There seems little doubt that it would add fun and excitement to an otherwise dull and dreary week. However, the thought of either having to live with this secret for the rest of one's life or having to tell it to a spouse, and facing certain displeasure and possible retaliation is enough to tip the scales in favor of resisting the temptation. From the perspective of projected retrospect, it is clear that long-term fulfillment is more important than a short-term fling.

Or suppose a couple is trying to decide whether to move to another city where the husband is offered a better job or to stay put for another year so that the wife can complete academic work essential to the development of her career. There is no doubt that they would be better off financially for the next few years if they were to move. The wife sometimes feels sick of school anyway, and on bad days she thinks it might be nice to give up the career, settle down, and raise a family. But as they imagine themselves ten years later looking back at this decision, they are both certain they would regret it. Therefore, they decide that long-term fulfillment requires a decision to stay.

In terms of the broad lines of our most important decisions and total style of life, it is wise to project ourselves to the end of life and to view our present way of living from that perspective. We may then decide that the rat race really isn't worth it or that it is better to spend our money for the down payment on a home or for regular weekends away together than to buy a new luxury car.

The Options Are Open

The "What's-right?" approach does not impose pre-assumed solutions on any problem. Because the husband is offered more money at a new position in a different city, it is not taken for granted that the couple will automatically pack up and move. More money is only one factor in the decision. The wife's employment, relationships with friends, educational and cultural opportunities for all the family, and many other factors may be of equal or far greater significance. It is necessary to weigh them all in attempting to decide the best course of action.

When operating with the "What's-right?" procedure, some decisions will be easy. The answer will often seem obvious, and mutual agreement will be almost instantaneous. But sometimes much study and discussion will be necessary before a consensus is reached, and on occasion husband and wife will arrive at diametrically opposed conclusions. The husband may be convinced that the offered promotion is the "chance of a lifetime" and that he would be crazy to turn it down. The wife may feel that a move to that city will make it impossible for her to complete her education and will destroy her lifelong dream of a personal career.

What should they do? We don't know, but we don't think either should automatically give in to the authority or pressure of the other. Have they fully explored all the possibilities? Are they objective about the facts of the matter? Would it be impossible for the wife to complete her education in the other city? Is his job offer really "the chance of a lifetime?" For mutual personal fulfillment are they able to endure being apart for a while? If one must sacrifice, for whom is the sacrifice less severe? To keep the decision focused on "What's the best course of action?" it may be helpful to bring in an objective person or couple—not to make the decision but to clarify the issues and weigh the alternatives.

Through this process one course of action will usually emerge as at least slightly preferable to the others, and both can agree that this, while painful, is best. Both will feel the pain and neither will be only capitulating to or "lording" it over the other.

But if, after careful study and objective conversation, he still says, "I'm going to move and take the job," while she maintains, "I'm going to stay and pursue my career," they have obviously agreed to separate temporarily at least and must next decide what this means for their marriage. If the choice of temporary separation reflects the value each places on career fulfillment and is not just a power play to coerce the other, it may be a responsible decision. To say this is not to degrade the value of the relationship but only to face the fact that marriage is based upon mutual respect and love. It gives neither husband nor wife the right to coerce or enslave the other.

Times to Give In

There are times when one will choose to give in to the other even when convinced that the partner is wrong. None of us is perfectly reasonable. We all have a capacity for stubbornness. Given this fact, we need to see each issue in light of the worth of the total relationship. If the wife is convinced that the family should go out for supper and the husband, seeing the refrigerator full of leftovers, is sure that dinner out is a wasteful extravagance, it may be wise for one to yield quickly and quietly to the other without going to war over it. If the husband loves his wife and is financially able to take her out, he will put her needs and desires above the cost of the dinner. If the wife knows the dinner out will necessitate dropping plans for a concert her husband deeply desires to attend, she will warm up the leftovers.

Such mutual consideration is part of the compromising that enables persons in love to live together harmoniously across the years. To give in under pressure alone may be a sign of weakness, but to give in out of love and wisdom is a mark of strength. Persons secure in themselves don't need to be right on every issue, nor do they stubbornly insist on everything going their way. "Love ... does not insist on its own way" (1 Cor. 13:4-5) but gives consideration to the needs and feelings of others.

Such love gives people room to make their own mistakes and to act in ways prompted more by emotional desire than by rational thought. This does not mean love itself is irrational, but it sees the emotional needs of life to be of great importance. They must be given at least equal consideration alongside the rational factors. For example, to squelch a partner's need for creative, cultural, or recreational expression because it's more rational to invest the money in the stock market may in the long run be as foolish as it is cruel.

Acting with loving consideration for another person's feelings does not mean being a puppet at the end of that person's strings nor a doormat over which others are welcome to walk. Every virtue needs to be balanced by its opposite virtue. Unselfish concern for others needs to be balanced by a proper respect for oneself. Spouses who always give in because of love may build a reservoir of resentment that may eventually be more destructive to the marriage than the momentary conflict from refusal to yield to the partner's every whim.

So even as there are times to give in, there are times to stand firm. One of the true marks of maturity is to have the love and wisdom to know the one from the other. We have no magic means of gaining that knowledge, but we are sure that commitment to "What's right?" rather than "Who's right?" combined with sincere respect for one's own and for each other's personal needs, brings a couple a long way toward maturity. Wisdom and love are the dominant factors in decision making.

Look for Specific Solutions

One thing we have learned through painful experience is that it is usually better to seek a specific solution to the problem at hand rather than gripe about each other's faults. If the husband persists in leaving his dirty socks on the bedroom floor, it can be an occasion to remind him, "You are the sloppiest man on earth." To really do such fault finding right, the wife will be sure to say, "Your mother picked up after you for years and spoiled you rotten, so it's no wonder you never grew up." Such comments will likely do nothing to improve the marriage or to move the socks.

Many wives, remembering that they have some habits that are irritating to their husbands, will solve the problem by simply picking up the socks themselves. Others may put a "socks box" in the closet and suggest that the husband, who has always been a hotshot basketball player, prove his skill by tossing his socks into the box. He may reply, "I'll do that if you'll stop leaving all your junk on the bathroom sink." Such willingness to work out an arrangement of "I'll do something for you if you do something for me" is a necessary part of civilized living together.

There may be truth in the suggestion that a good marriage is about 90 percent cooperative business arrangement and about 10 percent love and romance.

Contract to begin each day with courtesy. We can't become *perpetually* kind by willing to be so, but most of us can manage fifteen or twenty minutes in the morning. Being good to each other, or at least refraining from being unkind, during those morning minutes when we may feel sleepy and irritable, can set the stage for a better day for everyone.

As a general rule, it is unwise to make major decisions in a state of emotional distress. Unless you are both serene and happy in the morning, the time between bed and departure for work is usually better spent in positive anticipation of the possibilities of the day than in bickering over the problems of the past or present.

Postponing discussion of touchy subjects can, of course, lead to the avoidance of such conversation altogether. If we are to set times when we will not talk about certain things, we may need to be equally firm in contracting for specific occasions to hear each other out. Instead of doing the slow burn for days or weeks because he or she "never brings it up" or "obviously doesn't want to talk about it," the silence is better broken by saying, "I need to talk with you." Then proceed or set a time to do so.

There are people who have such great difficulty in deciding anything that they opt for almost perpetual indecision. Some seem to live in the hope that problems will go away. Others assume the role of a child and look to the father-husband or mother-wife to make the decisions. Then they complain that their partners are running their lives.

To decide to do nothing is, in effect, to choose to let things go on as they are. While it is sometimes wise to postpone making a decision, indecision is often the worst decision of all. Each of us needs to be occasionally reminded that we live in a real world where hard decisions must be made. We cannot live together in marriage as equally responsible adults while expecting the other, or permitting ourselves, to make all the decisions.

When Habits Clash

The principle of looking for a specific solution is especially helpful in dealing with the adjustments related to different styles of living. A husband, for example, may be extremely neat and orderly. He can't stand living with mess and disorder. Just walking into a room with newspapers haphazardly tossed on the furniture or toys strewn on the floor makes him uncomfortable. His wife, on the other hand, is a little ill at ease when everything is properly in place. She doesn't even notice the so-called mess he complains about. She likes the house to look "lived in," and picking up once a week or before company comes is sufficient for her.

To avoid endless frustration and bickering, some mutual accommodation is obviously necessary. Recognizing their differing attitudes toward neatness to be part of individual personality makeup, rather than conscious attempts to bug each other, they are free to concentrate on solving the problem itself. Their solution may require that the husband do the vacuuming once a week if the wife will pick up the newspapers before supper. They may also teach the children to return their toys to the toy box before going to bed.

Or suppose the husband is a night owl and his wife likes to go to bed with the chickens. By ten P.M. his head is alive with hopes of zestful romance, and she is ready to collapse. If he yields to her suggestion, "Let's wait till morning," the situation may then be reversed. Rested and refreshed, the wife is ready for an exciting start to the new day, but now he is so "conked out" he can hardly wake up in time for work, to say nothing of anything else.

It takes creativity, love, and patience to reach a mutually satisfying accommodation in such circumstances. Hopefully, there is some time during the day or night when they are both together and awake at the same time. When such times are limited, care must be taken to preserve these precious moments as islands of intimacy in all its dimensions. What a shame to waste them through preoccupation with details of traditional routine.

Right after dinner may be the usual time to wash the dishes, but this could be done later by the night-owl husband or the next morning by the early-bird wife so that they could have freedom for a couple of hours of early evening intimacy, best enjoyed with the door locked and the phone off the hook.

5

Alone Together

The responsibilities and distractions of parenthood often conflict with the intimacy needs of marriage. The fun time after supper often has to give way to the needs of a crying child. But don't give up. Try to find times and places to be husband and wife as well as father and mother. Just because something is difficult doesn't make it impossible. If children come to so dominate the home scene that little intimacy is possible, arrangements may need to be made to get away for regular weekends together. Some couples have a standing arrangement to care for each other's children a weekend a month so that each couple will have at least that much time alone together.

As we think of our dual roles as spouses and parents, we are reminded that some people become so possessed by their roles as father and mother that they cease to speak to each other as persons. We realize that in speaking with a child it is natural to say, "Mother wants to see you" or "Daddy would like you to help him," but we urge you to call each other by your own names, rather than address each other as "Mother" and "Father." Be persons and not just roles to one another.

When a couple lives with in-laws or shares housing with others, the preservation of privacy is especially difficult. Such arrangements may be temporarily necessary, but we believe every couple should endeavor to have their own home or apartment. When there are children, a lock on the bedroom door is a minimum necessity, and a room arrangement in which the couple need not fear being overheard is highly desirable. In our opinion, most homebuilders have given too little attention to this need. If planned into the home, privacy can be economically provided.

Speaking of Sex . . .

We believe that, at best, sexual relations can be one of the most significant "sacraments" of married love. There are certainly many other sacramental moments in marriage—mealtimes, playtimes, tearful times, times of laughter, times shared with close friends, times for going on a date together—but sexual relations are a special means of saying, "I love you" and "I want you to love me." These tender moments can renew the relationship and give deep personal satisfaction to both partners. In our opinion, sex is the wonderful gift of a loving God. He has endowed us with this capacity and desire not only, or even primarily, for the creation of children, but for our mutual joy.

In spite of (or is it sometimes because of?) all that has been printed and pictured about sex in recent years, misunderstandings still seem to abound. Many, for example, apparently think that sex appeal is a physical aspect that can be measured with a tape measure.

While appreciating the beauty of a shapely lady or the build of an athletic man, we are convinced that the sexiest part of our bodies is above the neck. The eyes, the voice, the facial expression, the thoughts, the words—these above all are the marks of a "sexy" man or woman.

Other physical attributes contribute or detract, and we should do all that we can to maintain our physical health and appearance, but they are usually of secondary importance. A sexy mind is more important than a sexy body. Because many fail to realize this fact, they are unnecessarily depressed over self-diagnosed lack of attractiveness. Others are deluded into thinking a well-endowed body alone gives them special sex appeal. Sex appeal, sexual ability, and sexual satisfaction have only limited relation to physical factors. Learning this can enhance self-esteem and heighten sexual fulfillment.

As in other areas of married life, our best advice here is to "be good to each other." Treat each other with tenderness and affection. Here, as everywhere, do what you can to give happiness, pleasure, and joy to each other. There will be times when you will not be particularly interested in the sexual invitations of the other, but you will not harshly push each other aside. In love you will sometimes permit what you did not desire and often be surprised by joy. At other times, the same love will restrain your desire so that you will not attempt to coerce or ridicule your partner.

Bed and Breakfast

Someone has said, "What happens at bedtime is often determined by how a husband and wife treat each other at breakfast." This is not to suggest a calculated breakfast ritual intended to pay off later, but is, rather, to emphasize the fact that our specific sexual experiences are always related to all the other dimensions of our total relationship. Some people who treat their spouses with indifference and disrespect all day wonder why their sexual overtures are rejected at bedtime. It would actually be surprising to be otherwise. How can persons whose minds are filled with bitterness and resentment freely and fully give their bodies to each other in the abandonment of sexual love?

This is not to suggest that sexual overtures are always out of place when resentments exist. The prelude to sexual relations in these circumstances can include conversation that opens the way to a sexually sacramental reunion of minds and hearts as well as bodies.

As what happens at breakfast influences what happens at bedtime, so also what happens at bedtime, or in bed before breakfast, influences what happens at breakfast and through the rest of the day. Our lives are a complex tapestry with many strands woven together. Each aspect of life affects all the others. For example, trouble with in-laws can disrupt an otherwise beautiful sexual relationship, and persistent sexual frustration can cause resentments expressed in a big blowup over a visit from in-laws. Recognizing the interplay of all these factors helps us sort things out so that we can come to terms with our true difficulties rather than dealing only with symptoms.

It's Not Always the Same

We also think it's important to realize that the experience of sexual relations is not always the same. Sometimes it's like having a seven-course candlelight dinner. At other times it's more like going to McDonald's for a hamburger. But what's so bad about that? As we can enjoy and be refreshed by both McDonald's and the finest restaurant, we can also enjoy and be enriched by a great variety of sexual experiences. Remembering this can free a couple from preoccupation with achieving supreme ecstasy in every encounter. Sexual relations can be beautiful in moods of play and fun and in more serene times of tender love. But they are seldom lovely when regarded as a duty or a competitive sport. To think in terms of "scoring" or "keeping score" is destructive to a sexual relationship.

Don't Try So Hard

Trying hard to get aroused or to have an ultimate sexual experience is like trying to go to sleep. The more you try, the worse it is. Wouldn't it often be better for the insomniac to try to stay awake and for the unresponsive to try not to get turned on? At least we seem to sleep best and respond most naturally when no one, including ourselves, is telling us we have to do so. A couple's bedroom should be free from demands, a place of rest and refreshment, a place to relax and enjoy being together.

In sexual relations as everywhere else, God invites us to live "by grace." We are to trust more than try, being open to receive gifts beyond our achieving. Grace doesn't demand anything. It doesn't say, "You must do this or that," but rather, "This is my gift to you." Sexual response is not something we achieve by our own effort. It is a gift of love received from our lover. Gerhard Frost's insightful poem speaks volumes:

Making love,
the ultimate frolic,
is the art of being second;
you dare not be good to yourself
until you've been good to the other.

55

Nourished, and sometimes saved, by a sense of humor,
love is the horizon of all that's human,
forever beyond our grasp, never fully attained.
(Seasons of a Lifetime, Augsburg, 1989)

When we concentrate on what *we* ought to do or feel, our attention is distracted from the very stimulation that can produce the responses we so desperately seek. We find the most fulfillment when we approach our sexual experiences without demanding anything of ourselves or each other. We don't even need to feel obligated to have sexual relations. Returning at times to the romantic patterns of courtship without intercourse can be meaningful for all of us. Don't miss the joy of just being close and tender with each other.

Some men seem to need assurance that tenderness is a masculine emotion. As a matter of fact, it takes a real man to be tender and affectionate. There are apparently some women who love to be overwhelmed by brute force, but as we understand it, the famous lovers of history are not the caveman types, but are those who know how to be sincerely kind and considerate. Consideration expresses an honest concern for someone else. Sexual love is more than an unselfish caring for another person, but it is never complete without it. In your sexual intimacy, as in hundreds of other ways, we hope you will both be strong enough to be tender and affectionate with each other.

Laugh at Yourselves

Another key ingredient is a sense of humor. We need to laugh at ourselves and to chuckle together over our blunders and clumsiness. We do not endorse ridicule or cynical, sarcastic humor. That can be disastrous to a sexual relationship. Put-down humor has no place in our life together. But we should not take ourselves too seriously, either. With good humor we can be free and playful without fear of being insulted or put down.

We don't recommend that you take a copy of the latest how-to-do-it book along on your honeymoon. Save that for later—maybe even five, ten, twenty years later. Do your own exploring and experimenting. Making your own discoveries will be more interesting and exciting. As you are able to leave your inhibitions behind, lovingly and playfully explore the dimensions of sexual love. You will likely have many years for such exploration. You don't need to try everything the first week you are married. Take time to learn what pleases each other.

There's an old story that some think illustrates the frequency of sexual relations in marriage. A supposedly wise father told his son, soon to be married, that if he puts a bean in a jar for each time he and his wife have intercourse during their first year of marriage and after the first year removes a bean for each sexual encounter, the jar will never be empty.

We emphatically disagree. Without having taken any scientific surveys, we believe that most healthy couples will empty the jar in only slightly more time than it took them to fill it and that there will be no dramatic decrease in the frequency of sexual relations at any point in their marriage. Although a gradual lessening is to be expected, this decrease in quantity may be more than compensated by an increase in quality. As with other great arts, the beauty of sexual relations can be increased with understanding, love, and much practice.

Speaking of such a lifelong honeymoon prompts us to add a word concerning the traditional honeymoon period that usually follows the wedding. Those days were wonderful for us, but we certainly don't regard them as "the best time of our lives." There are those for whom they are not wonderful at all. Few institutions are as overloaded with expectations as the honeymoon in particular and sex and marriage in general. Especially here patience, long-term perspective, and a sense of humor become of tremendous importance.

Regarding honeymoon trips, we urge that couples not attempt to see the whole world, but rather, plan for lots of leisure to just enjoy being together. On the other hand, doing nothing but being together can also wear thin, so seeing a little of the world might round out a beautiful time together.

If You Have Problems

We don't anticipate your having any serious problems in your sexual relationship and don't want you to worry about having them. We are grateful for having been so naive when we got married. We didn't even know what the potential problems might be! If you have read some of the literature that now abounds on this subject, we urge you to forget it. Be good to each other, laugh at your blunders, and 99 percent of the problems will solve themselves.

But if difficulties in this or any other area persist and threaten your personal fulfillment or continued relationship, don't endure them in resentful silence. Even if it is painful, share your concerns with each other. If this is not sufficient to resolve the difficulty, seek a counselor who can provide helpful information and insight.

We should treat ourselves and our marriages at least as well as we treat our cars. None of us would let a new car with a mechanical problem sit at the curb for six months without doing anything to repair it. Yet many live for years with personal and marital problems and do nothing to correct them. Each new day is full of potential for renewal of life, and we sometimes need a bit of outside help to discover and experience it.

Part of your marriage commitment might be spelled out in a specific contract in which you agree to seek help on those problems you are unable to resolve by yourselves. If a marriage is going to work, both husband and wife have to work at it. One spouse can kill a marriage, but it takes two to keep it alive and healthy.

6

Getting Out of Old Ruts

*S*omeone has described a rut as a grave with the ends knocked out. There can be times in marriage when we seem to be living in that kind of rut. There are no special problems, no crisis over which to contemplate divorce or murder, but we feel the old spark is gone. Everything is so daily. We are only going through the motions. When these times come, we are up against something which may be the number one enemy of joyful marriage. Its name is not crisis or conflict but boredom.

We can often manage the major crisis situations quite well. When illness strikes or financial disaster threatens, we rise to the challenge and work together with a sense of meaning and purpose. Our situation may be like that of a person who reported that, while huddled in a London bomb shelter during World War II, he suddenly realized he had very few problems.

When survival is at stake, most of our more petty problems suddenly disappear. But when we resume the regular routine, they usually reappear (though hopefully, in better perspective), and we must again deal with them. Among the most difficult of these is the sometimes deadly effect of the routine itself.

Battles with Boredom

The problem of boredom is especially difficult when it afflicts only one partner. She is perfectly content and considers the marriage the most satisfying experience of her life while he feels that life together is dull as dust. Or he may be the one who can't believe his wife is bored with a relationship that seems so good to him. In the extremes of these differences of feeling one may say, "I'm sorry, but I can't stand to live with you any longer" while the other says, "I love and need you so much, I am not sure that I can live without you." This is an extremely painful situation.

Fortunately, when boredom is involved, the intense feelings don't develop overnight, and there are things we can do to deal with them. Some are simple but significant, such as giving each other freedom to plan things we do together. When one is bored, it is usually because that person feels stifled and unfulfilled. We seem to be trapped. We see no way out. Facing that fact and looking together for ways to get out of the old ruts, and then caring enough to follow through on them, often is enough to give new meaning to the relationship.

In Each Other's Shoes

But the only way this can happen is for each of us to practice the ancient but difficult art of standing in each other's shoes. He may feel that a weekend away is a waste of time and money, and she may think that his idea of having some clean fun by taking a shower together is downright silly. But if they really care for each other and are concerned with each other's happiness and fulfillment, they will not lightly brush such suggestions aside. We do not advocate exorbitant waste nor continually silly behavior, but there are times when a little wastefulness and some frivolous abandonment brighten the day and add zest to living.

Jesus praised the woman who wasted costly ointment in an expression of lavish love (Matt. 26:6-13). His reaction invites us to be at least a little lavish in our expression of love to one another.

On a more profound level, boredom probably reflects unfulfilled expectations of the marriage and of each other. If these expectations are unrealistically excessive and would be unfulfilled in any marriage with any person, we need to come to terms with them. We may not be as bored with the marriage as with life itself, and especially with ourselves. We may need personal renewal, not a new spouse. Honest self-examination of our basic values and goals in life can be an occasion to seek new avenues of personal, vocational, and spiritual fulfillment.

Times to Play

We once heard a lecture for engaged and married couples entitled "Married for Keeps" and subtitled "Facts for Fumblers Frankly Faced." One of the speaker's suggestions was that wives and husbands occasionally play a game of tiddly-winks on the living room rug before going to bed. The purpose of this is to get couples into a playful mood as a prelude to what might happen in bed. Whatever its significance for bedtime, that advice has great importance for the rest of the marriage.

Without some kind of playful renewal, marriage can settle into a routine of working, eating, sleeping, and even making love that can become dull and lifeless. There is a child within each of us who wants to sing, dance, and play. This child needs room to run, but some marriages are so grim and serious that the poor child within is nearly stifled to death. Our hearts go out to such couples, wishing that somehow they might feel once more the joy of running barefoot in the sand and sense again the thrill of playful, tender love.

Heavy responsibilities and serious concerns demand our time and attention. But we can't live well under perpetual pressure. Therefore, we need frequent occasions of getting away from it all to be renewed in our persons and in our relationship. Jesus took time to enjoy flowers and be apart in a quiet place. If we get busier than he was, we are likely too busy for our own good or the good of others.

When All Else Fails

What if the expectations were realistic but are being increasingly unfulfilled? Is all lost and hopeless, or can the spirit of courtship be revived? The fact that the relationship was once exciting enough to lead to marriage holds promise that it can be so again. To face and confess feelings of disappointment costs some pride and risks resentment. But this is another essential part of the painful price of intimacy.

You may discover that your apparently contented partner isn't so content after all and that you are both open to deeper dimensions of sharing, which can transform boredom into meaning and joy. If you can't communicate these feelings alone together, the presence of an understanding counselor may help you share them and explore possibilities for new beginnings.

If through all this everything fails and you come to the honest conclusion that the marriage is dead, there may be no alternative in love or wisdom but to have a funeral for it. We do not advocate separation and divorce, but we are realistic enough to acknowledge that mutually destructive marriages devoid of possibilities for healing are better ended than prolonged. But such a decision should not be made lightly or in a fit of anger. Persons contemplating divorce face an awesome decision and need to sincerely ask, "Is this what we really want?" "Will this solve our problems?" "Is there nothing further we can do to renew our relationship?"

Some divorces lead to positive new beginnings for everyone involved, but in others people may go "from the frying pan into the fire." Perhaps it seems out of place to think of these things in a letter like this, but in a society in which thousands of marriages end in divorce, realism seems to demand it. Putting divorce into perspective now may eliminate the necessity of thinking about it later.

7

Concerns from Kids to Kinfolk

*U*ntil recently nearly everyone assumed that every couple would have children if physically possible. The fact that we can no longer take this for granted seems to us a sign of more responsible parenthood. We love our children and thank God for them. At the same time we believe that parenthood should be freely chosen and properly planned for.

There are some whose only family planning is, "We will have as many children as God gives us." To us this seems as irresponsible as a person raising rabbits saying, "I will raise as many rabbits as God gives me" without giving adequate consideration to how to feed and care for them.

God gives us more than sexual desire and the physical potential for parenthood; he also gives us the intelligence and the responsibility to live as wise stewards of all his gifts. As we rightly thank God for our sexual powers, we also thank him for ways of being more responsible in their use. Even as a couple can thank God for the joy and pleasure of sexual relations, they can also thank God for the pills and other means of contraception that give them the freedom to share their love sexually without fear of unwanted pregnancy.

The possibility of unhealthy side effects from some birth control methods must, of course, be considered, and a medical doctor is best qualified to advise on these matters. But morally, we believe their use to be a blessing for which we thank God, not a sin to confess.

Do not take chances, thinking, "We can always have an abortion." In the first place, "we" don't have an abortion. The wife does. And it is never a pleasant experience. A wise wife and loving husband will never select abortion as their method of birth control.

Beyond such consideration, we consider abortion at best a tragic necessity. Our experience of having lost our first baby girl, who was born during the fifth month of pregnancy and lived only an hour, has no doubt deeply influenced our belief and feelings. The thought of deliberately ending the life of an unborn child is terribly disturbing to us and underscores our urging responsible contraception so that it will never be necessary to consider an abortion.

If it is responsible for some couples to decide to have no children, is it also proper for others to have more than two or three? We think you must make your own decision in light of your personal circumstances seen within the wider context of global population concerns. For an outside authority to decide arbitrarily that any particular couple must either limit or increase their number of children seems a denial of personal responsibility and freedom. The population-food crisis may become so severe that this freedom will be no longer possible. But we hope that worldwide assumption of personal and social responsibility will make such legalistic birth regulation unnecessary.

Then There Is Money

There is an old saying, "It's no sin to be poor, but it's a terrible inconvenience"—and that's a fact! Is it also true, as D. H. Lawrence is reported to have said, that "a woman who is in love with a man will sleep on a board"? Will a man in love with a woman be as content with as little? Just how important is money in a marital relationship?

It seems to depend on the couple. If one or both are more in love with money and things than with each other, a situation of rivalry can occur, threatening the marriage as much as an outside lover. The husband who cares more for his car than for his wife, and the wife who regards her house as a greater treasure than her husband, are in a shaky marital situation.

In our experience, the quality of our relationship has been much more important than the amount of money in the bank. We come from families of limited means, simple tastes, and frugal habits. But we have been spared extreme poverty. We have also had many rich educational and cultural opportunities. We can't say how our marriage would have thrived under adverse conditions, but we are sure that if either or both of us were to live in ways that kept us on the verge of bankruptcy, it would hurt our relationship terribly.

Our money problems have stemmed more from management than amount. We share the same checking account and sometimes get into trouble by failing to record all the checks. There have occasionally been intense differences over specific spending decisions. One of us considers a certain expenditure an urgent necessity; the other sees it as a wasteful luxury or believes the money would be better used for something else. But thus far we have been able to arrive at mutually acceptable agreements or compromises.

Keeping our financial records has been mainly Carol's responsibility, but this is entirely a matter of personal agreement, ability, and interest. Most couples are wise to plan a budget together with equal regard for the needs and desires of each partner. Both should have some freedom to make individual purchases, but major items should be mutually decided upon. If you have limited experience with family budgeting, you may want to sit down with someone who can help establish a procedure to guide you.

Discipline is required to escape the temptation to fritter away our money on things that have no significant or lasting value. If we want to be rich, we may best become so not by securing everything we selfishly want but by reducing our wants to our needs. When we have all we need, what more do we need?

Money has been described as "our time and talent in portable form." Our money is an extension of ourselves. We use it most wisely when we spend it for our good and the good of others. One millionaire said, "I never had any fun with my money until I began to do good with it." His experience again witnesses to the fact that we find fulfillment in life when we give ourselves away in love to others.

In marriage, as in other human relationships, it is extremely doubtful that we can long enjoy luxuries for ourselves while we refuse to provide necessities for others. Be honest in sharing your true needs with each other, and try your best to put first things first. With regard to spending both money and time, we need to distinguish between the "musts" and the "maybes" in life. When there is a choice to be made, the rent must be paid, and the sailboat will have to wait.

What about Work?

During our thirty years together, we have experienced three of the most common marital work arrangements: only the wife working while the husband completed school; only the husband working while the wife was busy with babies, homemaking, and completing additional education; and both husband and wife working full time. Each stage has had its special joys and problems, but all things considered, we would do it that way again. We are intrigued, however, by some of the new arrangements, such as husband and wife each working half time. We hope that the business world will become increasingly open to this possibility so that couples will have more opportunity to share their lives with each other and with their children.

When the wife is working outside the home or has a virtually full-time job in caring for young children, the husband will see that sharing household duties is not doing her a favor but fulfilling his own responsibility. In this situation the specific housework assumed by each partner will depend upon personal interest and abilities. Talk it out and divide the work as fairly as you can. A clear understanding of mutually accepted responsibilities helps to avoid repeated resentment and continual conflict.

Don't nag each other about what's not being done. Face the tasks at hand and work out specific contracts for their completion. Then keep your commitments to each other as you would if they were made to someone else. If this becomes impossible, renegotiate the contract. Don't let it die by default. If one arrangement is bad, work toward another that is better.

Having Friends

We especially enjoy getting together with other couples and have always been grateful that we are enough alike to appreciate each other's friends. It has often been true that just spending an evening visiting or going to a movie with another couple has helped to renew us personally and to refresh our relationship with each other.

Others tell of special problems in this regard. One may be so attached to old friends that the other becomes jealous and resentful, or both may seek fulfillment so completely in each other that they cut themselves off from others. We hope that you will be able to share old friends together *and* be open to new relationships. Don't just "stew in your own juice." Invite others to share their life ventures with you, and be open to share yours with them. Doing so can be therapeutic and fulfilling for everyone involved.

In our marriage each of us also has a number of friends and co-workers with whom we share certain concerns that are not of interest to our spouse. Because we are secure in our relationship, these have never been a threat to us. They are, rather, another reminder that it is not possible for us to be everything or everyone to each other. We shouldn't even try. Even as we remain husbands and wives after becoming fathers and mothers, we also remain persons after becoming husbands and wives. We need freedom for nonromantic friendships which enable personal fulfillment beyond the gifts we can give each other.

Being Alone

Even as we stress the importance of having mutual and personal friends, we also need to give each other freedom to be alone. In the total rhythm of life, times of solitude and socializing alternate. The fact that each of you will continue to desire to do some things by yourself rather than together is not the sign of a bad marriage. Just as we need each other, we also need times and places to be alone with our own thoughts and to pursue our personal interests.

A husband who feels rejected because his wife would rather read a book than spend the evening with him watching TV, or the wife who thinks her husband is short on love because he prefers to work in the shop or garden than accompany her shopping, may need to ask if they are becoming excessively possessive. Refusing to watch TV together or retreating to the shop may be signs of rejection but may just as likely be signs of legitimate longings for personal fulfillment that are properly achieved alone.

Getting Along with In-laws

Persons soon to be married sometimes reply to inquiries about how they expect to get along with in-laws by saying, "I'm not marrying his or her family; I'm marrying him or her." While literally true, this isn't the total truth. For better or worse we marry into each other's families, and while in-law jokes abound, this fact is sometimes no joke. Difficulties seem to arise from two sources (often from both at the same time): the attitudes and actions of anxious overprotective parents and the attitudes and actions of immature, insensitive, defensive children.

Wise parents will give their adult children freedom to make their own mistakes, remaining available for support and guidance. Wise children will learn that it is often difficult for parents to achieve a proper balance in this regard. For parents to see someone they love following a road they are convinced leads to misery and regret and to be told to mind their own business is exceedingly painful.

A common fault of parents and spouses is the failure to realize that suggestions often imply criticism. When we frequently suggest, "Why don't you do it this way?", the other person may be hearing, "I think you are too stupid to know how to do anything right." Then, surprised that our kind and innocent suggestions are met with resistance and hostility, we defend ourselves by saying, "I am only trying to be helpful," which the other person may process as, "I am strong, wise, and helpful; you are weak, foolish, and much in need of my help."

The ability to give and receive suggestions depends largely on whether it falls within an essentially adult-adult rather than parent-child relationship. Understanding parents recognize that suggestions imply criticism and make them sparingly. They prefer to offer some tentative alternatives for action and leave the decisions to those who must live with them. Insightful children also recognize that there are many ways in which they need to learn and be helped. They are not too proud to receive an idea or a gift from parents.

Immature wives and husbands, who are insecure in the newly won freedom of adulthood, find it especially difficult to accept advice or counsel from their parents. Some are so defensive that they are offended by the most wise and helpful suggestions. Often they do the opposite, even to their own hurt, just to prove their independence.

We hope that you are mature enough to listen to advice from others, including your parents, to weigh it carefully, and then do what seems best to you. Do not let any outside person, be it parent or peer, run your lives. Remember again, it is not a question of "Who's right?" but of "What's right?" When a parent gives you an excellent idea, be mature enough to take it, but if it's a lousy idea, be smart enough and strong enough to reject it firmly and kindly.

Since parents are usually more willing to accept opinions from their offspring than from a son-in-law or a daughter-in-law, we suggest that if serious conflicts arise, you each take the central role in dealing with your own parents. It takes skill and patience to be firm in rejecting a parental viewpoint without rejecting them as persons. When they see that you appreciate their concern and respect their counsel even when rejecting it, they will likely grow in ability to let you make your own decisions.

If you have come through some painful cross-generational tension during adolescence, you may be surprised to begin to enjoy your parents' presence and to discover that they seem, for the first time in years, to be doing the same. You have moved out of the parent-child situation into a new relationship of adult-adult encounter in which you meet as equals. While this shift is never total, it can be the basis of mutual understanding and joy for both generations.

As you marry into each other's families, you also marry the family within each other. Even if you are thousands of miles away from your nearest relatives, you are never far from the family patterns that have become a part of each of you. What seems, for instance, to one of you the only way to celebrate Christmas may seem foreign to the other. The "child of the past" who lives within each of us longs for the familiar and may feel at home with some things the "adult of the present" professes to dislike. An awareness of this can make it easier for you to talk about your differences and adjust to them as you develop your own patterns of living.

Into the Wider Family

Whether we realize it or not, each of our small family units is part of a much wider extended family for which we have some personal responsibility. This family consists not only of blood relatives and in-laws, but also fellow citizens in our local community and wider world.

It is possible to become so involved with the political and social concerns of the community and nation that we neglect our responsibilities to spouse and children. But the opposite is also true: we can be so preoccupied with the inside business of the little family circle that we neglect our wider responsibilities to the community at large. When this happens, it too may be detrimental to our personal relationships with husband, wife, parents, and children.

Here again it is true that we find our lives by losing them. If our total concern is to save the marriage and create a happy family, we may be so self-preoccupied and self-centered that we become increasingly difficult persons with whom to live. We all need to get out of ourselves and to find reasons for living beyond our personal or family self-preservation.

A wise counselor once suggested to a troubled person, "Find someone who needs you and then give yourself to help that person." When we are excessively wrapped up in ourselves, we would do well to follow that advice. In one sense, the most important people in the world for each of us are not just those whom we need, but those who need us. Some of these are within the intimate circle of the little family, but others are served through agencies of church and community. As we give ourselves to this service, we not only help others but also discover new meaning for ourselves.

We especially urge you to seek friendships with persons in the older generation. There is sometimes less of a gap between grandparents and grandchildren than between parents and children. The idealism of youth and the wisdom of age can enable a meeting of hearts and minds that surprises both. Old age ensures neither insight nor maturity, but we think that you will be enriched by exploring the possibilities of cross-generational giving and receiving. If there is some kind of Friendly Visitor program in your church or community that could bring you into specific relationship with a senior citizen or two, we encourage you to become involved.

8

Faithfulness in Equal Marriage

*P*erhaps it's obvious by now that we affirm the basic tenets of equal marriage that seek to ensure personal fulfillment within the context of married love. In a healthy marriage individuality and mutuality go together. We saw a beautiful symbol of this fact at a recent wedding. The lighting of a "unity" candle is a common practice in weddings today. At the beginning of the ceremony, there are two candles burning at the front of the church with an unlit candle standing between them. After speaking their vows, the couple lights the center candle from each of the ones already burning. However, in this case the couple did not, as we sometimes see, blow out the individual candles. Doing so, it seems to us, would be a sign of individuality going up in smoke. As the three candles continued to burn, it was a symbol of both the mutuality and the individuality, the unity and the diversity that characterize mature marriages.

While endorsing the basic principles of equal marriage, we do not believe it is possible to have stability without a solid foundation of trust and faithfulness. It is one thing to say, "I'll attend the Bach recital while you are at the rock concert," but quite another to say, "You can go to bed with anyone you desire, and I'll feel free to do the same." As we need room to grow in our personal interests, we also need limits to maintain the relationship.

In marriage we make a basic commitment of faithfulness to each other. We give ourselves to be special to each other. We declare each other to be first in our love and trust. As it is logically impossible to have two best friends or two highest loyalties, we can't have a primary love commitment to two people at the same time. There are some who believe it is possible to maintain a basic love commitment while allowing all manner of extra-marital relationships, but we are either too old-fashioned or too wise to believe that. We cannot be special to each other while sharing everything with someone else.

Sacramental Sex

We know that life is an exceedingly complex business and do not wish to judge others whose views or styles of living are different from our own. But we are convinced that sex is special. This is a fact not just of our culture but of our creation. Music is for public consumption; sex is for private communion. We believe that sexual relations are meant to be the personal sacrament of each marriage. To share this gift with others is to undercut the foundations of the relationship and to cheapen the gift itself.

Sexual promiscuity either before or during marriage is as unwise as it is immoral. Some say that a couple should test their sexual compatibility before marriage, but this kind of evaluation may be similar to testing a parachute by jumping from a fifth-story window. The conditions need to be right. In terms of sexual fulfillment that, for us, means the existence of a secure relationship of love and commitment. "Testing" compatibility introduces elements of insecurity and fear of failure which undermine the test itself. Similarly, if promiscuity in marriage is sinful, it is also unwise and hurtful. One person's evaluation of an extra-marital affair was not "How could I have been so sinful?" but rather "How could I have been so foolish?" Others regard their affairs differently and may view them with gratitude, but we believe that they destroy the marriage relationship and in the long run have more potential for misery than for joy.

To Be Trusted

While stressing sexual fidelity, we realize that there are hundreds of other ways to break faith with each other. We could fall so in love with our work, our money, our golf game, bridge club, or even our children, that we have little time to care for each other. Some who develop an unhealthy dependence on alcohol or drugs are actually involved in a chemical love affair in which preoccupation with the chemical overshadows and threatens all other relationships. We could lie, deceive, and mislead in ways that make it next to impossible for us to trust each other. Trust is created by the persons in whom we have it, and while it takes much time to build, it can be quickly destroyed. As you wish to be trusted, seek to do everything you can to enable your partner, and everyone else for that matter, to trust you.

There may be some rare circumstances in life when it's necessary to lie to preserve a life (as when a World

War II family told the Gestapo they had not seen the American paratrooper hidden in their home), or to keep a confidence (as when quizzed about information you have pledged to keep secret), but we should avoid deception, including white lies and half truths that undermine our ability to trust each other. Open sharing of the essential truth is a vital component of healthy marriage.

A Faith to Share

Along with everything else, we are grateful to have been able to share a common faith and united experience of worship. We believe that God loves us even more than we love ourselves or could ever love each other. He has promised to love us forever. We have done and will do many hurtful things, but in Jesus Christ we still dare to trust that nothing we have done or can do will ever stop God from loving us. As it is not possible for us to stop the sun from shining, so also we believe that it is impossible for us to stop God from loving us. This shared faith continues to give strength and meaning to our lives. Beyond this message of God's gracious love and power, central to trust and hope, we are also continually refreshed by the human relationships within the wider family of our community of faith.

Both of us have come from homes in which Christian faith seemed a natural part of the fabric of life, but in neither of these families was there an abundance of religious ritual or legalistic rigidity in belief or behavior. We were encouraged to live with trust in a gracious God who expresses the love and mercy exemplified by Christ. We were taught to live with love toward people who, however much we might dislike or differ from them, were as loved and valued by God as we were ourselves.

We do not know how our children will someday look back on the spiritual dimension of our family life together, but our hope for you, as for them, is that you will be enabled to live your lives in trust of God and love of people and that you will be able to share this dimension of depth and height with one another.

Reverence the Mystery

As you live in trust of God, you will be constantly called away from the idolatrous worship of each other about which we warned you earlier. At the same time you will experience an increased reverence for the mystery of life you encounter in yourselves and in each other. After years of marriage which will tempt you to believe you can read each other like a book, you will often be surprised by mystery that will make you say, "I couldn't understand you fully if we lived together for a hundred years." And it will be true. Each of us human beings is a miniature world of mystery, perhaps more complex than all the physical universe.

Being unable to fully comprehend our wives or husbands should not surprise us, for in fact we do not understand ourselves very well. We often wonder, "Why did I do that?" or "How could I have forgotten?" or "What makes me feel this way?" We are a mystery to ourselves as well as to one another.

A sense of mystery and a bit of awe in each other's presence makes life a more exciting adventure. In our marriages such reverence for the mystery of life keeps us from settling down in the dull satisfaction of having arrived. In marriage, as in all of life, we never arrive; we are always on the way. We are on the move, hopefully, toward total marriage and total joy. But we always fall far short of it. As the beauty of the swift sparkling stream far exceeds the sight of a stagnant pond, so the

83

gladness of life venturing, risking, stumbling, and rising to move on again far exceeds the joy of life at rest. Thus may each day for you be an adventure of new beginning—a day full of danger and full of hope, a day full of grace and by that grace a day of life abounding.

The Best Year of Your Lives

Some time ago we received a letter from E. Stanley Jones which concluded with the words, *May you have the best year of your lives.* This is our final wish for you as you begin your married life together, and on every wedding anniversary we renew that wish for each new year ahead.

Having begun early in this letter by warning you to prepare for the worst, we end by urging you to be open to the best. Each of us needs some place to be at our worst, and home is probably the safest place for that. But home is also a good place for us to be at our best. Within the safety of marriage, you are free to give yourselves to each other in the abandonment of love.

Look for the best in each other, share your best with each other, give your best selves a chance to flower and to grow. You have potential for pain (we have said enough about that), but you also have great potential for pleasure and joy. God in love wills to bless you and to give you life in all its fullness. May you so live in that love that your lives together will be to God's glory and to your great joy.

With love,
Aunt Carol and Uncle Lowell

Questions for Reflection and Discussion

THESE QUESTIONS are intended to encourage communication between men and women planning or experiencing marriage. In order to stimulate focused discussion between engaged couples and spouses, and to facilitate concrete as well as comprehensive discussion in groups, the questions are presented under eight themes expressing some of the most important concerns of married or engaged couples. Page numbers refer to relevant sections of *Be Good to Each Other*.

A. On Expectations (pp. 11-16):

1. What are the most significant characteristics of good and bad marriages?
2. What do a husband and wife have a right to expect of each other? What have they no right to expect?
3. What does a couple have a right to expect of marriage? What have they no right to expect?

4. What portion of life's troubles and joys do you think come from being married? From factors unrelated to marriage?
5. What do you consider the most significant factors contributing to fulfillment or lack of fulfillment in marriage? Why are these so important?
6. In what specific ways can realistic expectations help us avoid unnecessary frustration and disappointment?
7. How can we help each other to have more realistic expectations of marriage? of ourselves? of each other?
8. What can we do to help make our most positive expectations come true?

B. On Communication (pp. 17-28):

1. If it is true that to love is to share what is in your deepest heart, what do we have to share? Is it all good and beautiful?
2. Why do you think that it is so difficult for us to share the best and the worst of what is in us?
3. Do you agree that each of us yearns for a relationship in which we can be open and honest with each other? What can be done if one hungers for such sharing but the other fears or feels little need of it?
4. Do you think that the mental and emotional intimacy of sharing mind and heart brings us even closer together than the physical intimacy of sexual relations? Why?
5. Some who claim to love truly find it difficult to say, "I love you." What do you think accounts for this? What can be done about it?
6. Can you give specific examples of ways by which we cut off communication with each other? of ways we help each other to be more expressive?

7. What are the dangers of relying on reading each other's mind? To what extent is verbal communication necessary? When is it enough to let our attitudes and actions speak for themselves?

8. What is the significance of questions such as "What do you mean?" and "What are you trying to tell me?"

9. Try using some of the communication starters such as "I like it when . . ." (p. 21). Can you suggest other specific means of increasing concrete communication?

10. Should a couple tell each other everything? When? Why? Why not?

11. Do you agree that it is best to "accentuate the positive?" Can we do so and yet be honest? How?

C. On Being Good Friends (pp. 29-38):

1. How important is it to marry a good friend? What are the characteristics of such friendship?

2. What is the significance of mutual respect? To what extent is it important that marriage be a partnership of equals?

3. Why is pity a poor basis for marriage?

4. In what ways is it possible to treat one's spouse as a kind of god? Why do you think this happens? In what ways is it dangerous? How can we correct such attitudes?

5. What is your opinion of marriages in which one or both are committed to changing the other? Does acceptance or coercion make constructive change more likely? When is coercion necessary?

6. To what extent are "the pains of intimacy" a part of every relationship in depth? How can we help ourselves and each other endure these pains constructively?

7. Could you be content with a good business-part-ner-type marriage without the intimacy of close friendship? Explain.

8. What will result if both husband and wife think most about what they can get from, rather than give to, each other?

9. To what extent should "I'm sorry, Honey" be part of the language of marriage? What effects does such confession have? Can it be overdone?

10. How can vicious cycles of meanness be broken and new cycles of kindness be started? Can you give examples?

11. Is it possible to live without angry and hostile feel-ings toward each other? What happens when we try?

12. What is the difference between saying, "You make me angry!" and "I am angry"? How can we confess more of our own feelings and accuse or attack each other less?

13. What are the most constructive ways of handling hostile feelings? the most destructive? How can we express our anger more constructively?

D. On Decision Making (pp. 39-50):

1. Do you believe that the husband as "head of the house" has the right to make all major decisions?

2. Do you believe that a wife who lets her husband make all major decisions gives up something es-sential to her whole personhood?

3. Should husbands and wives give each other the right to make decisions in certain areas? Is such an arrangement the complete solution to problems of decision making?

4. Do you agree that it is better for husbands and wives to think in terms of "What's right?" rather

than "Who's right?" What are the advantages and disadvantages of this procedure?

5. Which of the tests of right and wrong on pp. 41-42 seem most important to you? Can you give examples of their use? Can you suggest other tests?

6. In what circumstances is it wise for a husband or wife to give in to the other? When is it unwise? What are the possible consequences of either action?

7. Why is it more helpful to concentrate on specific problems and possible solutions than to complain about each other's faults?

8. When is it wise to postpone making a decision? When is it unwise? What can a couple do when one or both can't make decisions?

9. What place do contracts that say, "I'll do something for you if you will do something for me" have in marriage?

10. Is the "What's right?" rather than "Who's right?" approach in harmony with biblical passages such as Genesis 1:26-31, 2:18-25; 1 Corinthians 14:34-36; Galatians 3:27-28; Ephesians 5:21-33; 1 Timothy 2:8-15; and 1 Peter 3:1-7? Which of these most clearly express the gospel of Christ, and which are more expressive of the culture and customs of that time?

11. Compare Ephesians 5:21-33 with Ephesians 6:5-9. If we do not understand 6:5-9 as an endorsement of slavery for all time, is it also possible that we need not understand 5:21-33 as an endorsement of male-dominated marriage for all time? Why?

E. On Sexual Fulfillment (pp. 51-59):

Discuss the truth or falsity of the following statements:

1. The most important purpose of sexual relations is to have children, the next is to express love, and

the third is to enjoy personal pleasure.
T____ F____

2. First Corinthians 7:5 teaches us that sexual relations are not just for the purpose of having children.
T____ F____

3. Desire for sexual fulfillment is the number one reason for getting married. T____ F____

4. Persons having strong sexual attraction for each other are most likely to have a successful marriage.
T____ F____

5. Persons with little sexual interest in each other should not get married. T____ F____

6. Men are much more interested in sex than women.
T____ F____

7. Women are capable of greater sexual satisfaction than men. T____ F____

8. The test of a sexual relationship is its effect upon the total person. T____ F____

9. Couples should not have sexual relations unless both are equally interested. T____ F____

10. It is the husband's responsibility to initiate sexual overtures and the wife's to say yes or no.
T____ F____

11. During sexual relations, the husband should be active and the wife passive. T____ F____

12. Christians are forbidden from engaging in other than "standard" sexual activity. T____ F____

13. It's perfectly all right for Christian couples to do anything sexually which they both desire and enjoy.
T____ F____

14. It's sinful for a Christian couple to watch an X-rated movie together. T____ F____

15. The frequency of sexual relations decreases dramatically after the first year of marriage.
T____ F____

16. Many healthy couples continue an active sex life into their sixties, seventies, and eighties.
    T____ F____

17. Genesis 1:27, 31 and 2:24-25 teach us that sex is good. T____ F____

18. Since sexual relations are a sacramental gift from God, Christian couples should enjoy them often.
    T____ F____

19. The Christian doctrine of grace contradicts attitudes that regard sexual relations as a duty or that demand performance from oneself or each other.
    T____ F____

20. The message of grace invites us to approach each other in love without demanding anything of ourselves or each other. T____ F____

21. Since most sexual problems can't be solved anyway, there is no use to talk with anyone about them.
    T____ F____

22. In a fully open marriage, couples who love each other will give each other freedom to have sexual relations with whomever they wish. T____ F____

23. Extra-marital affairs are not just against the Bible but against marriage and against each other.
    T____ F____

24. Premarital sexual relations are okay between persons who really love each other. T____ F____

25. Couples who really love each other will refrain from sexual relations before marriage. T____ F____

26. One of the problems with premarital sexual relations is that they tend to short-circuit the relationship and hinder the development of friendship.
    T____ F____

27. God did not give us the commandment forbidding adultery because sex is evil but because it is good.
    T____ F____

28. The purpose of the commandment forbidding adultery is to help ensure sexual fulfillment and to preserve the family. T____ F____

29. Jesus' statement that "everyone who looks at a woman with lust has already committed adultery with her in his heart" (Matt. 5:28) condemns all sexual desire. T____ F____

30. Sexual desire is a gift of God and is as normal and good as blood pressure or hunger for food. T____ F____

31. Lust is not the same as sexual attraction. T____ F____

32. Words as well as actions are a very important part of a sexual experience. T____ F____

33. All experiences of sexual relations are about the same. T____ F____

34. Since sex is serious business, there is no place for humor in sexual relationships. T____ F____

35. Some kinds of humor destroy a sexual relationship. T____ F____

F. On Getting Out of Old Ruts (pp. 61-65):

1. Can you give examples to illustrate boredom and its effects in marriage?

2. What do you consider the most significant factors contributing to boredom in marriage? the factors preventing boredom?

3. How important is it for both husband and wife to plan activities together or take turns in planning them? In what ways can contracting to do so be helpful?

4. Is it better to confess feelings of boredom to each other or to seek excitement elsewhere?

5. To what extent should we do things which are enjoyable and exciting to our partners but seem unnecessary or silly to us?

6. If honest self-examination reveals that we are bored with ourselves and life in general and not just with

each other, what can we do to discover new meaning and joy in living?

7. What is the importance of play in our personal and married lives? What can we do to enable and increase playfulness?

8. What is the significance of periodic weekends away together? How can these be economically arranged?

9. In what circumstances should a couple seek outside counsel to improve their marriage? When first married, should every couple promise each other to seek outside counsel before filing for separation or divorce?

10. When is a husband or wife justified in seeking separation or divorce?

11. When contemplating separation or divorce, of what significance are such questions as "Will this really solve my problems?" "Is this what I really want?" "Is there nothing further we can do to renew the relationship?"?

12. What more might church, school, and state do to make divorce less necessary?

13. Are divorce and remarriage of divorced persons in accord with biblical passages such as Matthew 5:31-32; Matthew 19:3-12; Mark 10:2-12; Luke 16:18; and 1 Corinthians 7:10-11?

14. Read Jesus' words, "Not everyone can receive this teaching, but only those to whom it is given. . . . Let anyone accept this who can" (Matt. 19:11-12). Does this mean that Jesus' prohibitions of divorce and remarriage of divorced persons are not universal laws for all people for all time?

15. What are the implications of the Christian gospel of grace for specific decisions concerning divorce and remarriage of divorced persons?

G. On Relationships beyond Each Other (pp. 67-77):

1. Is it wrong for a couple to decide never to have any children? to have more than two or three children?
2. Are physically safe means of birth control a gift from God for which we give him thanks and praise?
3. When and why is abortion justified? When and why is it not justified?
4. Are children always a blessing to marriage?
5. How important is money in a marital relationship?
6. Should every couple have a specific budget, or is it enough that expenditures don't exceed income?
7. When both husband and wife work, is it better to keep separate accounts or to put the money together and have joint checking and savings accounts?
8. When both work, to what extent should they share household responsibilities? How are these best arranged?
9. Of what importance is it to have outside friendships with individuals? with other couples? Are there dangers?
10. What are the most difficult problems in getting along with in-laws? What are the best ways of handling these problems?
11. Do you agree that if serious conflicts arise with in-laws each of you should take the central role in dealing with your own parents?
12. Are your in-law problems caused by overprotective, domineering parents or by defensive, insecure children? What can be done to establish a more adult-adult relationship?
13. If suggestions often imply criticism, can you illustrate some of the best and worst ways of giving advice?
14. Of what significance to marriage are relationships beyond the family circle?

H. On Faithfulness and Faith (pp. 79-84):

1. To what extent do you agree with the principles of "equal marriage"? Give examples to illustrate your views.
2. In what ways is it sometimes necessary to sacrifice personal fulfillment for marital fulfillment? marital fulfillment for personal fulfillment?
3. What is special about sexual relations? Can they be shared with others without damaging the marital relationship?
4. In what ways other than sexual infidelity can a husband and wife be unfaithful to each other?
5. What is necessary in marriage to enable a couple to trust each other? Do you agree that trust is created by the persons in whom we have it?
6. Are there times when it is best for couples to withhold the truth or lie to each other?
7. In what ways does the mystery of each other's presence add frustration or fascination to marriage?
8. How important is it for a couple to share the spiritual dimensions of life? What are some of the better ways of handling the adjustments of a religiously mixed marriage?
9. Is it possible to share a common faith while belonging to different churches? What attitudes are essential to such a situation?
10. Is retreating into religious indifference a realistic solution to problems of religious differences?
11. Can you suggest specific means by which a couple can more fully share the spiritual dimensions of life?
12. In what ways can a couple enable each other to look forward to sharing the coming years together?